LOS ANGELES
DODGERS

by Marty Gitlin

Published by ABDO Publishing Company, 8000 West 78th Street, Edina, Minnesota 55439. Copyright © 2011 by Abdo Consulting Group, Inc. International copyrights reserved in all countries. No part of this book may be reproduced in any form without written permission from the publisher. SportsZone™ is a trademark and logo of ABDO Publishing Company.

Printed in the United States of America,
North Mankato, Minnesota
112010
012011

Editor: Chrös McDougall
Copy Editor: Nicholas Cafarelli
Interior Design and Production: Kazuko Collins
Cover Design: Craig Hinton

Photo Credits: Al Behrman/AP Images, cover; AP Images, 1, 4, 7, 9, 12, 15, 16, 19, 21, 24, 26, 28, 31, 42 (middle, bottom), 43 (top); Bain News Service, 10, 42 (top); Hulton Archive/Getty Images, 23; Yarnold /AP Images, 32; Michael Caulfield/ AP Images, 34, 43 (middle); Rusty Kennedy/AP Images, 36, 43 (bottom); Lenny Ignelzi /AP Images, 39; Jeff Chiu/AP Images, 41; David Zalubowski /AP Images, 44; Mark J. Terrill/AP Images, 47

Library of Congress Cataloging-in-Publication Data
Gitlin, Marty.
  Los Angeles Dodgers / by Marty Gitlin.
     p. cm. — (Inside MLB)
  Includes index.
  ISBN 978-1-61714-048-8
  1. Los Angeles Dodgers (Baseball team)—History—Juvenile literature. I. Title.
  GV875.L6G58 2011
  796.357'640979494—dc22
                              2010036567

TABLE OF CONTENTS

CHAPTER 1

FINALLY!

I t did not seem to matter when the Brooklyn Dodgers won 98 games and the 1955 National League (NL) pennant. It did not seem to matter that pitcher Don Newcombe compiled a brilliant 20–5 record that year. It did not seem to matter that outfielder Duke Snider smashed 42 home runs or that the team led the NL in every important offensive statistical category.

The Dodgers were bound to lose to the New York Yankees in the World Series. They had always lost to the Yankees in the World Series. They had fallen to the mighty American League (AL) champions in 1941, 1947, 1949, 1952, and 1953. So when the 1955 World Series began,

Hot, Hot, Hot

The 1955 Dodgers ran away with the NL pennant right from the start of the regular season. They won their first 10 games and soon had a 22–2 record. By June 23, the Dodgers owned a 49–16 mark. They coasted the rest of the way and won the title by a whopping 13½ games.

Dodgers pitcher Don Newcombe brought a 20–5 record into the 1955 World Series against the New York Yankees.

the Dodgers fans in Brooklyn, New York, awaited the inevitable. When their beloved team lost the first two games of the Series at Yankee Stadium, that fear only grew.

But suddenly the Dodgers came to life. They won their next three games at home at Ebbets Field. Snider and catcher Roy Campanella combined for five home runs. The Yankees rebounded to win Game 6. But the Dodgers had a chance to make up for all their losses to the Yankees by winning the do-or-die Game 7 at Yankee Stadium.

The Dodgers entered the bottom of the sixth inning with a 2–0 lead. They were led by the brilliant pitching of left-hander Johnny Podres. Then the Yankees put two runners on base with nobody out. Yogi Berra sliced a long line drive down the line. Dodgers left fielder

Right Move, Right Time

Dodgers Manager Walter Alston inserted Sandy Amoros into Game 7 of the 1955 World Series at the ideal moment. Amoros did not start the game because the Yankees started a left-handed pitcher. However, he replaced Jim Gilliam in left field in the sixth inning. That was just in time to catch the line drive off the bat of the Yankees' Yogi Berra and save two runs from scoring. It is generally accepted that the right-handed Gilliam would have never caught up to that ball.

Sandy Amoros sprinted 150 feet into the corner and made a spectacular catch. He then turned and fired the ball back into the infield. Shortstop Pee Wee Reese caught the ball and caught the runner off first base for a double play. The rally was squelched.

That was all Podres needed. He completed the 2–0 shutout to give the Dodgers their World Series title.

Pitcher Johnny Podres gets a lift from catcher Roy Campanella after the Dodgers won Game 7 of the 1955 World Series.

The win set off hysteria in the New York borough in which the Dodgers resided. Wrote one Brooklyn fan after the triumph, "It was our national pastime (as the phrase goes) at its best. And the underdog, Brooklyn—beloved, bedraggled, un-glamorous Brooklyn, always the also-ran, the runner-up, the butt of jokes—emerging bloody, bowed, but victorious after so many long years."

The celebration in Brooklyn lasted well into the night. It was a moment captured by *Sports Illustrated* writer Robert Creamer.

"[O]n the night of October 4 in the year 1955, there really was dancing in the streets of Brooklyn, and weeping for

DUKE SNIDER

New York baseball teams featured some of the greatest center fielders in baseball history during the 1940s and 1950s. The Dodgers were no exception. Duke Snider starred for the Dodgers from 1949 to 1962.

During that time, Snider both scored more than 100 runs and racked up more than 100 runs batted in (RBIs) six times. He led the NL in runs scored three times, hit 40 or more home runs every year between 1953 and 1957, and earned spots on the NL All-Star team in seven straight seasons. Snider was also a top fielder with a strong and accurate arm.

"No player contributed more to our team both offensively and defensively," wrote Dodgers pitcher Carl Erskine. "No player agonized more when he didn't perform well. Could he have been better? Some say yes. I say they didn't know him the way I did." Snider was inducted into the Baseball Hall of Fame in 1980.

pure joy, too," he wrote. "For that was the day the Dodgers at long, long last brought the baseball championship of the world home. . . . Hundreds crammed into the ancient Hotel Bossert on Montague Street to help the Dodgers celebrate. Thousands more milled around outside, cheering, yelling, dancing."

The Dodgers were great again in 1956. Newcombe won a career-high 27 games that season. Meanwhile, Snider hit a career-high 43 home runs. The Dodgers swept a three-game series with the Pittsburgh Pirates to clinch the hotly contested NL pennant. That set up a rematch against a Yankees team seeking revenge.

The World Series proved to be a mirror image of the one played a year earlier. This time it was Brooklyn winning the

Dodgers outfielder Duke Snider (4) hit four home runs among his eight hits in the 1955 World Series.

first two, losing the next three and winning the next one to set up a Game 7 showdown. Yankees right-hander Don Larsen threw the only perfect game in World Series history in Game 5. But after the Dodgers won Game 6, the fans had reason to be optimistic. Newcombe would be pitching for them in Game 7. Meanwhile, the Yankees sent out 23-year-old Johnny Kucks.

But with the title on the line, Newcombe pitched poorly. Kucks, meanwhile, hurled a 9–0 shutout. The Dodgers had again lost the World Series to the Yankees. And after the following season, the team moved from Brooklyn to Los Angeles. All the loyal Dodgers fans had were memories. But they were some of the fondest memories any baseball fan could enjoy.

CHAPTER 2

THE FIRST DODGERS

Brooklyn baseball is about as old as the sport itself. The New York City borough fielded its first team in 1849. That team eventually played in the Interstate League and American Association. Its home field was Washington Park. That was near the location where George Washington's Continental Army fought the Battle of Long Island during the Revolutionary War.

The Brooklyn club debuted in the NL in 1890 by winning the pennant. That team boasted some top players. Tom Lovett became the only pitcher in team history to win 30 games. Tommy "Oyster" Burns led the league with 128 RBIs.

But the best player of that era did not arrive until 1893. His name was Willie Keeler. His .341 career batting average still ranks 14th in the history of baseball.

Another key person around that period was Charles Ebbets.

Charles Ebbets bought the Dodgers and built Ebbets Field, which was the Dodgers' home ballpark from 1913 to 1957.

Casey Stengel, *left*, spent the first six years of his playing career with the Dodgers. In 1934, he became manager of the team.

He began by selling peanuts and tickets at Washington Park and eventually purchased a small stock in the team. In 1897, he was named president of the team. Five years later, he used the money he earned as president to become its sole owner. In 1913, he bought land that was converted into a new home for his team called Ebbets Field.

The team had a breakthrough in 1914 when Wilbert Robinson took over as manager. The manager nicknamed "Uncle Robbie" made an immediate impact on the team, which became known as the Robins. He guided the team to a winning record in 1915 and to its first World Series in 1916. Pitcher Jeff Pfeffer won 25 games in 1916 as the team went 94–60.

The World Series itself did not go so well. Young outfielder Casey Stengel led the team with a .364 Series batting average, but Brooklyn lost to the Boston Red Sox in five games. The team returned four years later after holding off a late-season surge by the archrival New York Giants. But Brooklyn fell to the Cleveland Indians five games to two in the 1920 World Series.

"The Brooklyns played listlessly and at no time did they show any fighting spirit," wrote one *New York Times* reporter. "The marvelous pitching staff which brought the Dodgers to the National League pennant has made a sorry showing in this series."

Actually, it was the Brooklyn hitters who were more to blame. The team scored just eight runs in the seven-game series against the Indians.

Before the Dodgers

The Brooklyn baseball team was known by several different official and unofficial names before it permanently became the Dodgers in 1932. From 1888 until 1898 the team was known as either the Bridegrooms or Grooms. That was because seven players had gotten married around the same time. It was also known, at one time or another, as the Trolley Dodgers (for the trolley cars that traversed the city), Ward's Wonders (for manager Monte Ward), Foutz's Fillies (for manager Dave Foutz), the Robins (after manager Wilbert Robinson), and the Superbas (for a Brooklyn theater).

Some key players kept Brooklyn competitive for the next 15 years. Pitcher Dazzy Vance won 50 games between 1924 and 1925. Batters Zach Wheat and Babe Herman routinely batted around .300. But the team rarely contended.

The team came close a few times. It made a big September push in 1924 to make up 13 games and move into first place. But the Giants eventually came back to win. Brooklyn also won 11 straight games in 1930. That put the team atop the NL. But it struggled down the stretch.

The Robinson era ended in 1932. That is also when the team became officially known as the Dodgers. But the results under new managers Max Carey and then Stengel and Burleigh Grimes were disastrous. In 1938, however, an innovator named Larry MacPhail was hired as executive vice president. He would lead the team to a period of greatness both on and off the field.

MacPhail had introduced night baseball while with the Cincinnati Reds. He brought it to Brooklyn in 1938 by installing lights at Ebbets Field. A year later he hired Red Barber to call Dodgers games. Barber became one of the most famous radio broadcasters in baseball history. MacPhail's biggest success, however, was hiring Leo Durocher to manage the team. The outspoken manager would lead the Dodgers to seven winning seasons during his eight full seasons there.

By 1941, the Dodgers had stockpiled plenty of talent. One of those talented players was first baseman Dolph Camilli.

"Wee" Willie Keeler

When asked about his success as a hitter, Brooklyn outfielder "Wee" Willie Keeler exclaimed, "I hit 'em where they ain't." That is exactly what he did. The 5-foot-4 (1.63 m), 140-pound (63.5 kg) Keeler remained one of the top hitters in baseball for a generation. He played for Brooklyn in 1893, and again from 1899 to 1902. He had 200 or more hits and had more than 100 runs in eight straight seasons in Baltimore and Brooklyn. His .424 batting average in 1897 was among the highest in the history of the sport. Keeler finished his career in 1910 and was elected into the Baseball Hall of Fame in 1939.

Pitcher Dazzy Vance, *right*, shares the spotlight with Babe Ruth, *left*, at a media event late in his career.

He hit 34 home runs that season. Another, outfielder Pete Reiser, led the NL with a .343 batting average. Reiser and fellow outfielder Joe Medwick both scored at least 100 runs. Meanwhile, pitchers Kirby Higbe and Whit Wyatt combined for 44 wins. Wyatt posted a fine 2.34 earned run average (ERA).

Their strong performances resulted in a 100–54 record and the team's first pennant in 21 years. Awaiting them in the World Series were the New York Yankees. Pennants and showdowns against their hated AL rival were about to become quite familiar to the Dodgers and their fans.

CHAPTER **3**

COMING UP SHORT

The 1941 World Series was up for grabs. The Yankees won two of the first three games, but the Dodgers were on the verge of evening it up. They led 4–3 with two out in the ninth inning of Game 4.

Dodgers pitcher Hugh Casey then threw strike three to New York batter Tommy Henrich. But the ball slipped past catcher Mickey Owen. That allowed Henrich to reach base. Then the Dodgers imploded. Three hits and two walks later, they trailed 7–4.

"At 4:56 p.m. yesterday darkness and gloom came to Brooklyn," wrote *New York Times* sports reporter Louis Effrat. "This was no phenomenon, even though, the sun was still shining. After all, in a borough of nearly 3,000,000 persons whose daily happiness rises and falls with the fortunes of the Dodgers, one couldn't possibly expect sweetness and light after what had happened to The Bums in the ninth inning."

Dodgers fans affectionately knew their team as "The Bums." But after the team lost

Pee Wee Reese was named an All-Star ten times during his 16 years with the Dodgers. He also was known for befriending Jackie Robinson.

Game 4 and Game 5—and the Series—the nickname was uttered in anger.

The Dodgers finished second in 1942. Then the team lost several players to the military during World War II. After some down years, the Dodgers rebuilt a talented lineup. Veterans Pete Reiser and Dixie Walker combined with young players like shortstop Pee Wee Reese, second baseman Eddie Stanky, and outfielder Carl Furillo in 1946. They led the team to a tie for the NL pennant. But the Dodgers lost to the St. Louis Cardinals in a playoff.

By that time, the Dodgers had made headlines off the field. Racism and an unwritten code in baseball had prevented blacks from playing with whites

Pee Wee

Harold Henry Reese was known as "Pee Wee" throughout his career. He weighed just 160 pounds (72.6 kg), but he earned his nickname because of his skill in the game of marbles as a child. In fact, he won a marbles championship at age 12 in his hometown of Louisville, Kentucky. Despite his size, Reese exhibited good power. He hit 10 or more home runs in a season seven times in his career. He exceeded 90 runs scored in eight consecutive seasons and was in the top 10 in NL MVP voting on eight separate occasions.

in the AL and NL. That forced African Americans to play in the Negro Leagues. Dodgers president and general manager Branch Rickey believed that discrimination had no place in America. As such, he signed a young African-American player named Jackie Robinson to a contract before the 1946 season.

Carl Furillo practices catching a fly ball off the wall at Ebbets Field as stadium workers prepare the field for the 1956 World Series.

Robinson shredded minor league pitching in 1946. He had a .349 batting average. The Dodgers promoted him in 1947. Rickey knew that Robinson would face racism and taunting from the fans, players, and coaches. He believed that Robinson would be emotionally strong enough to handle that pressure.

"I'm looking for a player with enough guts not to fight back," Rickey said.

Robinson showed that he was able to handle those challenges. He also showed that he was a worthy major leaguer. Robinson led the Dodgers to the 1947 NL pennant. Batting second in the order, Robinson hit .297 with 125 runs scored and 29 stolen bases. That performance earned him Rookie of the Year honors.

The Dodgers, however, still had to face the Yankees

Jackie Robinson

Jackie Robinson was 28 years old when he broke the color barrier in Major League Baseball (MLB). But he sure made up for lost time. He batted over .300 in six consecutive seasons and scored more than 100 runs in six of seven years. He also led the NL in stolen bases in 1947 and 1949. But his statistics pale in comparison to the impact he had on American society. It has been claimed that the integration of baseball and his dignified handling of the racism and discrimination he faced helped pave the way for the civil rights movement of the 1950s and 1960s.

in the World Series. The Dodgers appeared doomed when they lost the first two games. But they battled back to win three of the next four and push it into a seventh and deciding game. And when they held a 2–0 lead in the second inning, they looked to be on their way to their first championship. But they were shut out the rest of the way. The Yankees won 5–2.

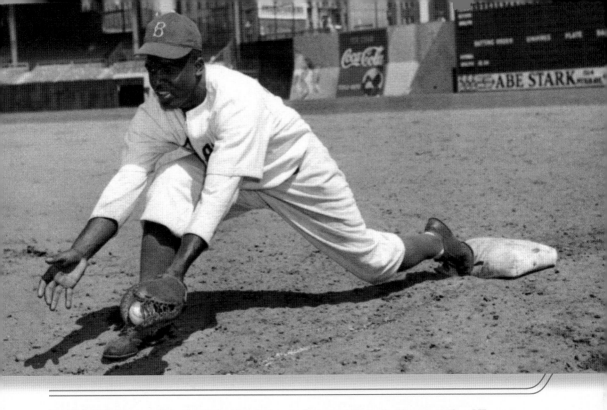

Jackie Robinson did not take long to make an impact. He was the NL Rookie of the Year in 1947 and the NL MVP in 1949.

Losing to the Yankees was becoming a recurring nightmare in Brooklyn. The Dodgers added catcher Roy Campanella in 1948. Then they added another star for the next season: pitcher Don Newcombe. The team had another great season in 1949. Robinson earned the NL Most Valuable Player (MVP) Award by batting .342 and scoring 122 runs.

Newcombe was voted Rookie of the Year after winning 17 games with a 3.17 ERA.

Manager Burt Shotton led the Dodgers to another NL pennant. But they could not overcome the Yankees in the World Series. The Dodgers won just one of five games in the 1949 Series.

The shock in 1951 was that they did not reach the World

A CLASSIC FALL CLASSIC

By 1953, the Dodgers had fallen to the New York Yankees four times in the past seven years. But the Dodgers never gave up in those Series. That was especially true in 1952, when they took the Yankees to a seventh and deciding game.

The Dodgers fell behind 4–2 in Game 7. In the seventh inning they loaded the bases with one out and the heart of the lineup looming. After Duke Snider popped out, Jackie Robinson hit what appeared to be a routine pop-up in the infield. But neither pitcher Bob Kuzava nor first baseman Joe Collins could locate the ball. If it dropped, the Dodgers would have scored three runs, taken the lead, and likely won the Series. But Yankees second baseman Billy Martin raced forward and snagged it just inches from the ground. Brooklyn did not score again. The Dodgers lost again to the Yankees.

Series. The Dodgers led the hated New York Giants by 13½ games in mid-August. They played better than .500 the rest of the way. But the Giants caught fire and tied Brooklyn by season's end. That forced a playoff series. The Dodgers led the third and deciding game, 4–2, in the ninth inning. But pitcher Ralph Branca surrendered a three-run homer to Giants batter Bobby Thomson to lose the pennant.

It also ripped the hearts out of the Dodgers. Pitcher Carl Erskine recalled the sad scene as his teammates returned to the locker room.

"I was conscious of being a part of history," Erskine said, "so I watched when all the guys came in. Jackie [Robinson] just slammed his glove hard into his locker. . . . [manager Chuck] Dressen tore off his uniform shirt so violently

Catcher Roy Campanella joined the Dodgers in 1948. He was named the NL MVP three times, in 1951, 1953, and 1955.

that his buttons flew around the room. And then [Branca] came in and sat on the steps leading to the training room, the big No. 13 on his back. Finally, his head dropped to his chest and his arms fell forward between his knees. There was bedlam [in the Giants clubhouse] next door, but our place was like a tomb."

It would be like a tomb again after they lost yet again to the Yankees in the 1952 and 1953 World Series. But at least Brooklyn had a baseball team at that time. By the end of the decade, the Brooklyn Dodgers were nothing but a memory.

CHAPTER 4

BYE, BYE, BROOKLYN

The Dodgers finally broke through with a victory over the Yankees in the 1955 World Series. Fans wondered if that win was the start of something great. Pitcher Don Newcombe helped the Dodgers answer that question. He became the first player to win the Cy Young and the MVP awards in the same year in 1956. That helped the team to another date with the Yankees in the World Series.

The Dodgers won the first two games at Ebbets Field. They even scored 19 runs in the process. Fans were starting to believe that they were on the verge of something big. But then the offense stalled. The Dodgers scored a mere six runs in the last five games of the Series. They scored just one in the final three games. The result was a heartbreaking seven-game defeat.

Dodgers fans would soon have more reason to feel heartbroken. Owner Walter O'Malley

Pitcher Don Newcombe spent seven and a half seasons with the Dodgers. In 1956, he won the NL MVP and Cy Young awards.

The Dodgers played their final game at Ebbets Field in Brooklyn on September 24, 1957.

had been seeking a new ballpark to replace Ebbets Field, which was falling apart. But city officials could not find a suitable site. Despite the team's success on the field, attendance was dwindling. Meanwhile, MLB wanted to relocate struggling teams to California. West Coast cities like Los Angeles

Game Over

Though relief pitchers received few accolades in baseball until the late 1970s, one Dodgers reliever played a huge role in their success a decade earlier. And that was Ron Perranoski. From 1961 to 1967, Perranoski racked up 101 saves and 52 wins out of the bullpen. He was spectacular in 1963, posting a record of 16–3 and a 1.67 ERA.

and San Francisco were going through a postwar population boom.

Loyal Dodgers fans could sense what was about to happen as every option to keep the team in Brooklyn fell through. Finally, on October 8, 1957, O'Malley announced that the Dodgers were moving to Los Angeles. Meanwhile, the New York Giants accepted an invitation to move to San Francisco.

Though millions in Brooklyn were sad, most believed it was justified economically. The reasons for the move were explained in a story published 40 years later in *Sports Illustrated.*

"O'Malley came to realize that Brooklyn in the 1950s was a changing and disintegrating community and that the essentially middle-class fans who supported the ball club were rapidly moving to the suburbs," wrote Robert Creamer. "The . . . children and grandchildren of the immigrants who had arrived in Brooklyn around the turn of the century were leaving . . . and while they continued to follow the Dodgers on radio and television and in the newspapers, they weren't as much in evidence at Ebbets Field itself.

"Their beloved stadium was a deteriorating antique with almost no parking for cars, and it wasn't all that handy to public transportation. Ebbets Field was an old-fashioned neighborhood ballpark that was losing

Tommy Davis led the NL with a .326 batting average in 1963 and helped the Dodgers win the World Series title that year.

its [fans]. . . . The Dodgers' park may have been lovably old, dirty, and decrepit, but it was not jammed to the rafters with cheering [supporters]."

They were jammed to the rafters in Los Angeles. And they had a wonderful team to cheer for. That was especially true in 1959. Gil Hodges, Jim

Gilliam, and John Roseboro all performed well that season. However, it was the pitching staff that truly dominated. Veterans Johnny Podres and Roger Craig combined with young pitchers Don Drysdale and Sandy Koufax to lead the Dodgers to the pennant. The team led the NL in attendance with more than 2 million fans.

Making matters worse for the jealous Dodgers fans in Brooklyn, this time they won the World Series. Relief pitcher Larry Sherry was the hero. He either won or saved all four victories over the Chicago White Sox.

Although the 1959 Dodgers pitching staff was good, it was still young and improving. By the early 1960s, Koufax and Drysdale had emerged as one of the most dominant tandems in baseball history. Koufax, in fact, developed into what many consider the best left-hander ever. From 1963 to 1966, he compiled a record of 97–27 with three 300-strikeout seasons. He also led the league in shutouts three times and never posted an ERA above 2.04.

In 1963, the Dodgers again had a chance to avenge all of those World Series losses to the Yankees. And this time they did it in a four-game sweep. Koufax, Drysdale, and Podres limited the Yankees to just four total runs. Young outfielder Tommy

WALTER ALSTON

Walter Alston was no baseball star. He played just one game in the major leagues and struck out in his only at-bat. But he sure was a successful manager. Alston took over the Dodgers in 1954 and led them to their first World Series title a year later. He guided the Brooklyn team to another pennant in 1956. Then he guided the team to three World Series titles while in Los Angeles.

Alston served as manager of the team for 23 years and suffered through just four losing seasons. He finished his career with a 2,040–1,613 overall record. His win total ranks ninth in major league history. After Alston died in October 1984, former Dodgers pitcher Don Drysdale spoke about his ability to get his points across to his players.

"He was the strong, silent type," Drysdale recalled. "But you knew darn well when he was mad. . . . Whatever you had done, you wouldn't do again."

Davis had led the league with a .326 average. He batted .400 against the Yankees. But when it was over, media members surrounded the brilliant pitching star.

"In the Dodger dressing room everyone wanted Koufax—radio, television, photographers, the press," wrote *Sports Illustrated* reporter William Leggett. "Tommy Davis stood with tears in his eyes deep inside his dressing cubicle. . . . Finally Koufax walked away from his pursuers and into Davis' cubicle. He threw his arms around Tommy, and Davis blurted out: 'Sandy, you are the greatest pitcher that ever lived!'"

Koufax was at least the greatest pitcher in baseball through 1966. He was a primary reason why the Dodgers beat the Minnesota Twins in the 1965

Dodgers pitchers, *from left*, Don Drysdale, Pete Richert, Stan Williams, Sandy Koufax, and Johnny Podres pose together in 1962.

World Series. He also helped the Dodgers win another pennant the following season, although they lost to the Baltimore Orioles in the Fall Classic.

When Koufax retired due to arthritis in his elbow after the 1966 season, the team's run of pennants was over. But not for long.

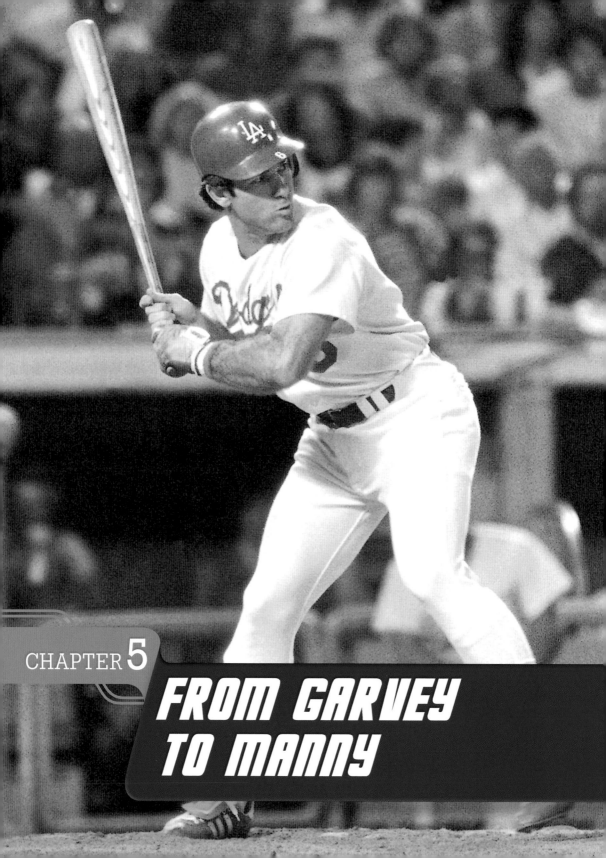

CHAPTER 5

FROM GARVEY TO MANNY

One sign of a successful team is that it remains a contender when players come and go. The Dodgers continued to win after ace pitchers Sandy Koufax and Don Drysdale retired. For a while, they just did not win as much. In the early 1970s, they generally finished behind the powerful Cincinnati Reds in the NL Western Division.

By that time, the Dodgers had restocked their lineup with talented players such as first baseman Steve Garvey, second baseman Davey Lopes, and third baseman Ron Cey. They also continued their tradition of strong pitching. The Dodgers featured veteran starters Don

Complete Player

Steve Garvey could hit for average and for power and was an excellent fielder. Garvey played for the Dodgers from 1969 to 1982, during which time he compiled 200 or more hits in a season six times and exceeded 100 RBIs five times. He was the 1974 MVP and won four consecutive Gold Glove Awards.

First baseman Steve Garvey was a 10-time All-Star and ended his career with 2,599 hits.

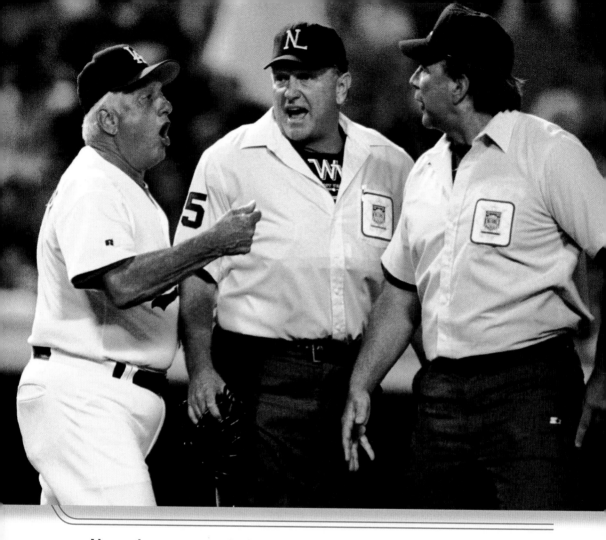

Always known as a colorful character, Tommy Lasorda, *left*, spent 21 seasons managing the Dodgers and won two World Series titles.

Sutton, Claude Osteen, Andy Messersmith, and reliable reliever Mike Marshall.

The addition of Jimmy Wynn—combined with the emergence of Garvey and Cey and a sensational season by Marshall—resulted in a 102–60 record and division title in 1974. The three sluggers averaged 24 home runs and 105 RBIs. Marshall shattered a major league record with 106 appearances and won 15 games out of the bullpen. Meanwhile, Messersmith and Sutton combined for 39 victories.

And when the NL Championship Series (NLCS) rolled around, they were ready. Garvey, Cey, and shortstop Bill Russell led the offense. Sutton was nearly flawless on the mound in shutting down Pittsburgh. The 1974 Pirates boasted one of the best lineups in baseball history.

The Dodgers lost the World Series to the Oakland Athletics. But they had served notice that they were among the elite teams in the NL. Meanwhile, manager Walter Alston announced that he would retire after the 1976 season.

The Dodgers did not miss a beat under replacement Tommy Lasorda. They won pennants in 1977 and 1978, beating the Philadelphia Phillies in the NLCS both years.

BLEEDING DODGER BLUE

Neither Walter Alston nor Tommy Lasorda were great baseball players. Lasorda pitched in 26 games and never won one. But both were Hall of Fame managers. Lasorda guided the Dodgers to eight first-place finishes and two World Series titles. He also personified the spirit of the team. "I bleed Dodger blue," he once said. "And when I die, I'm going to the big Dodger in the sky."

Lasorda was known for his positive outlook and being able to get the most out of his players. He finished his managerial career in 1996, having experienced just six losing seasons in 21 years. He was selected NL Manager of the Year in 1983 and 1988.

When he retired, the Dodgers had completed a 42-year period during which they had just two managers. Continuity at that position has been credited, in part, for the Dodgers' success.

Kirk Gibson's game-winning, two-run home run in Game 1 of the 1988 World Series is one of baseball's most memorable moments.

But those victories were followed by losses to the Yankees in the World Series.

The 1981 season was different. The regular season had been cut short by a work stoppage. It was also cut into two halves. The Dodgers won the West Division for the first half of the season and earned a spot in the playoffs. Then they beat the Houston Astros and the Montreal Expos to reach the World Series.

They played the Yankees again in the World Series. This time, though, the result was different. The Dodgers won four games to two. It was their first World Series title in 16 years. Three Dodgers players shared the Series MVP Award. Sluggers Cey, Pedro Guerrero, and Steve Yeager combined to hit .327 with five home runs and 17 RBIs.

As the decade progressed, the Dodgers became known as a team that contended for pennants but could not win them. They lost the division by one game in 1982 and fell in the NLCS in 1983 and 1985.

When the team suffered through rare losing seasons in 1986 and 1987, it appeared it was heading in the wrong direction. But behind strong seasons by outfielder Kirk Gibson and pitcher Orel Hershiser, the Dodgers dominated the NL West in 1988. Hershiser won the Cy Young Award with a 23–8 record. He even broke a major league record set by Drysdale 20 years earlier by pitching $59\frac{1}{3}$ consecutive shutout innings. Although he played hurt most of the year, Gibson still won the NL MVP Award.

Gibson won the award as much for how he inspired his teammates as for his production on the field. That inspiration was evident in Game 1 of the World Series, as the Dodgers played the heavily favored A's. The Dodgers trailed 4–3 in the bottom of the ninth. In from the bullpen strolled usually invincible A's closer Dennis Eckersley. He promptly retired the first two batters. After Mike Davis walked, Gibson limped to the plate as a pinch-hitter.

The veteran outfielder was not even supposed to play. His injured left knee and right hamstring were aching. He could barely walk. But on a 3–2 count, he yanked a line-drive home run into the right-field stands to give his team the victory. In one of the most replayed moments in baseball history, Gibson pumped his fist twice after rounding first base. The fans at Dodger Stadium went crazy. Everyone in attendance and watching on TV knew that they had witnessed one of the greatest moments in baseball history.

"The swing and the result are unexplainable," Gibson said years later. "Other than maybe to say it was destiny."

The Dodgers lost just one game in winning that World Series. And although that proved to be their last pennant or world title through the 2010 season, they continued to field strong teams. Talented players such as catcher Mike Piazza, first baseman Eric Karros, and

Slugging Backstop

The Dodgers selected Mike Piazza in the 62nd round of the 1988 amateur draft—number 1,390 overall. The pick was in some ways done as a personal favor, as Dodgers manager Tommy Lasorda was a friend of Piazza's family. But it turned out to be a good one. Piazza played for the Dodgers from 1992 to 1998, and batted at least .318 each season from 1993 to 1997. He was named Rookie of the Year in 1993 and is considered one of the greatest hitting catchers in baseball history.

Mike Piazza became one of the top hitting catchers during his six and a half years with the Los Angeles Dodgers. He was a five-time All-Star.

outfielder Raul Mondesi kept the Dodgers competitive in the 1990s. The team also had solid pitching in starters Ramon Martinez and Hideo Nomo and closer Todd Worrell. Although the Dodgers reached the play-offs in 1995 and 1996, they were never able to get past the NL Division Series.

The Dodgers only had three losing seasons between 1997 and 2010. But it was not until 2004 that they reached the playoffs again. That began a stretch in which the team won three division titles and a wild card in six years.

Much of that success was a product of good personnel moves. The Dodgers boasted one of the top farm systems in baseball. It produced young stars like first baseman James Loney, outfielders Matt Kemp and Andre Ethier, starting pitchers Chad Billingsley and Clayton Kershaw, and closer Jonathan Broxton. The team complemented those players with top veterans. Among them were shortstop Rafael Furcal, outfielder Manny Ramirez, and pitchers Derek Lowe and Brad Penny.

In 2008 and 2009 they reached the NLCS. Although they fell short of the World Series each time, the Dodgers upheld their tradition of excellence.

The more times changed the more they stayed the same. Years passed and the Dodgers even moved from the East Coast to the West Coast. But through it all, they remained one of the finest teams in baseball.

Players such as Reed Johnson, *left*, Matt Kemp, *center*, and Andre Ethier helped the Dodgers become contenders again during the 2000s.

TIMELINE

1890	The Brooklyn Bridegrooms join the NL and win the pennant in their first season.
1899	Brooklyn wins the first of two consecutive NL pennants.
1914	Wilbert Robinson is named manager and will remain at that post for 18 years.
1916	The Brooklyn Robins win their first pennant in 16 years, but lose to the Boston Red Sox in the World Series.
1920	The Robins fall to the Cleveland Indians on October 12 to lose another World Series.
1938	Larry MacPhail brings night baseball to Brooklyn by installing lights at Ebbets Field. The first night game is played on June 15.
1939	Leo Durocher is hired as the new Dodgers manager and guides them to the pennant in 1941.
1946	Jackie Robinson breaks the color barrier by signing a contract with the Dodgers. He reaches the big leagues in 1947 and becomes a star.
1954	Walter Alston is hired as manager and remains in that position through 1976.
1955	The Dodgers defeat the New York Yankees, 2–0, on October 4, to win their first World Series.

1957	Owner Walter O'Malley announces on October 8 that he is moving the team from Brooklyn to Los Angeles.
1959	The Dodgers clinch their second World Series title on October 8 with a 9–3 win over the Chicago White Sox.
1963	The Dodgers complete a four-game World Series sweep of the Yankees with a 2–1 victory on October 6.
1965	Sandy Koufax pitches a three-hit shutout on October 14 to give the Dodgers a 2–0 victory over the Minnesota Twins and the 1965 World Series title.
1977	Tommy Lasorda takes over as Dodgers manager from retired Alston.
1981	The Dodgers clinch the first of two World Series under Lasorda on October 28 with a 9–2 defeat of the New York Yankees.
1988	A dramatic home run to win Game 1 by Kirk Gibson on October 15 propels the Dodgers to a five-game World Series victory over the Oakland Athletics.
1996	Lasorda retires as manager and is replaced by former Dodgers shortstop Bill Russell, who guides the team to the playoffs.
2009	The Dodgers reach the NLCS but lose to the Philadelphia Phillies. It is the fourth time in six years that they reach the postseason.

QUICK STATS

FRANCHISE HISTORY
Brooklyn Bridegrooms (1888–98)
Brooklyn Superbas (1899–1910)
Brooklyn Trolley Dodgers (1911–12)
Brooklyn Robins (1914–31)
Brooklyn Dodgers (1913, 1932–57)
Los Angeles Dodgers (1958–)

WORLD SERIES
(wins in bold)
1916, 1920, 1941, 1947, 1949, 1952,
1953, **1955**, 1956, **1959**, **1963**, **1965**,
1966, 1974, 1977, 1978, **1981**, **1988**

NL CHAMPIONSHIP SERIES
(1969–)
1974, 1977, 1978, 1981, 1983, 1985,
1988, 2008, 2009

KEY PLAYERS
(position[s]; seasons with team)
Roy Campanella (C; 1948–57)
Don Drysdale (SP; 1956–69)
Steve Garvey (1B; 1969–82)
Willie Keeler (OF; 1893, 1899–1902)
Sandy Koufax (SP; 1955–66)
Mike Piazza (C; 1992–98)
Pee Wee Reese (SS; 1940–42, 1946–58)
Jackie Robinson (OF; 1947–56)
Duke Snider (OF; 1947–62)
Don Sutton (SP; 1966–80, 1988)
Dazzy Vance (SP; 1922–32, 1935)
Zach Wheat (OF; 1909–26)

KEY MANAGERS
Walter Alston (1954–1976)
    2,040–1,613; 23–21 (postseason)
Leo Durocher (1939–46, 1948)
    738–565; 1–4 (postseason)
Tommy Lasorda (1977–1996)
    1,599–1,439; 31–33 (postseason)

HOME PARKS
Washington Park (1884–90)
Eastern Park (1891–97)
New Washington Park (1898–1912)
Ebbets Field (1913–57)
Los Angeles Memorial Coliseum
    (1958–61)
Dodger Stadium (1962–)

* All statistics through 2010 season

QUOTES AND ANECDOTES

Through the 2010 season, the Dodgers had the most no-hitters in major league history with 20. They have been split evenly by Brooklyn and Los Angeles pitchers. Sandy Koufax and Carl Erskine are the two Dodgers who have thrown more than one, and only Koufax has hurled a perfect game. Koufax, who pitched one no-hitter every year from 1962 to 1965, retired all 27 Chicago Cubs in a 1–0 victory on September 9, 1965.

The game played at Ebbets Field on June 15, 1938, was noteworthy for more than the fact that it was the first one played at night at that historic venue. It also marked the second consecutive no-hitter thrown by Cincinnati Reds pitcher Johnny Vander Meer. Vander Meer blanked the Dodgers, 6–0, that night. He remains the only pitcher in baseball history to toss consecutive no-hitters.

The belief that the Dodgers could draw more fans in Los Angeles than they could in Brooklyn proved to be justified. The team drew nearly 2 million in its first season in Los Angeles in 1958 and exceeded that total for the first time in team history a year later. Since moving to Los Angeles, annual attendance has been higher every year than the best figure in Brooklyn Dodgers history. The Dodgers broke 3 million in attendance for the first time in 1978 and have exceeded that figure every year since 2001.

Outfielder Gary Sheffield played just three full years with the Dodgers—but what a great three years. He topped a .300 batting average, 30 home runs, and 100 RBIs all three seasons from 1999 to 2001. His best season was 2000, when he batted .325 with 43 home runs and 109 RBIs. Sheffield also walked 101 times that year.

GLOSSARY

accolade

A compliment or credit for a job well done.

attendance

The number of fans at a particular game or who come to watch a team play during a particular season.

borough

An area of New York City.

clinch

To officially settle something, such as a berth in the playoffs.

contend

To be in the race for a championship or playoff berth.

continuity

Remaining the same, without interruption.

farm system

A big-league club's teams in the minor leagues, where players are developed for the majors.

general manager

The executive who is in charge of the team's overall operation. He or she hires and fires managers and coaches, drafts players, and signs free agents.

pennant

A flag. In baseball, it symbolizes that a team has won its league championship.

rookie

A first-year player in the major leagues.

stock

A purchased share of ownership of a business or sports franchise.

veteran

An individual with great experience in a particular endeavor.

wild card

Playoff berths given to the best remaining teams that did not win their respective divisions.

FOR MORE INFORMATION

Further Reading

Eig, Jonathan. *Opening Day: The Story of Jackie Robinson's First Season.* New York: Simon & Schuster, 2008.

Johnson, Richard A., and Glenn Stout. *The Dodgers: 120 Years of Dodgers Baseball.* Boston: Houghton Mifflin, 2004.

Travers, Steven. *Dodgers Past & Present.* Osceola, WI: MVP Books, 2009.

Web Links

To learn more about the Los Angeles Dodgers, visit ABDO Publishing Company online at **www.abdopublishing.com**. Web sites about the Dodgers are featured on our Book Links page. These links are routinely monitored and updated to provide the most current information available.

Places to Visit

Dodger Stadium
1000 Elysian Park Avenue
Los Angeles, CA 90090
866-363-4377
http://losangeles.dodgers.mlb.com/la/ballpark/index.jsp
This has been the Dodgers' home field since 1962. Tours are available when the Dodgers are not playing.

Jackie Robinson Museum
1 Hudson Square, 75 Varick Street
New York, N.Y. 10013
212-290-8600
jackierobinson.org/about/museum.php
This museum centers on the achievements of Jackie Robinson, as well as the significance of his life.

National Baseball Hall of Fame and Museum
25 Main Street
Cooperstown, NY 13326
1-888-HALL-OF-FAME
www.baseballhall.org
This hall of fame and museum highlights the greatest players and moments in the history of baseball. Roy Campanella, Sandy Koufax, Jackie Robinson, and Dazzy Vance are among the former Dodgers enshrined here.

INDEX

About the Author

Marty Gitlin is a freelance writer. He has written more than 25 educational books. Gitlin has won more than 45 awards during his 25 years as a writer, including first place for general excellence from the Associated Press. He lives with his wife and three children in Ohio.